Down in the Jungle 1,2,3

A Rain Forest Counting Book

by Tracey E. Dils

AMICUS READERS 1 AMICUS INK

Say Hello to Amicus Readers.

amicus readers

You'll find our helpful dog, Amicus, chasing a ball—to let you know the reading level of a book.

1 Learn to Read

Frequent repetition, high frequency words, and close photo-text matches introduce familiar topics and provide ample support for brand new readers.

2 Read Independently

Some repetition is mixed with varied sentence structures and a select amount of new vocabulary words are introduced with text and photo support.

3 Read to Know More

Interesting facts and engaging art and photos give fluent readers fun books both for reading practice and to learn about new topics.

Amicus Readers and Amicus Ink are imprints of Amicus
P.O. Box 1329, Mankato, MN 56002
www.amicuspublishing.us

Library of Congress Cataloging-in-Publication Data
Dils, Tracey E., author.
  Down in the jungle, 1, 2, 3 : a rain forest counting book / by Tracey E. Dils.
    pages cm. -- (1, 2, 3... count with me)
  Summary: "Introduces rain forest plants and animals, such as orchids, jaguars, and snakes, while teaching the concept of counting to ten"-- Provided by publisher.
  Audience: Grades K to 3.
  ISBN 978-1-60753-715-1 (library binding)
  ISBN 978-1-60753-819-6 (ebook)
  ISBN 978-1-68152-001-8 (paperback)
  1. Counting--Juvenile literature. 2. Rain forest animals--Juvenile literature. 3. Rain forest plants--Juvenile literature. I. Title.
  QA113.D5526 2015
  513.2'11--dc23
                          2014045268

Photo Credits: Ralph Loesche/Shutterstock Images, cover (background); Shutterstock Images, cover (top left), cover (bottom left), 8, 10 (left), 11, 13, 14-15 (foreground), 14-15 (background), 16 (top), 16 (bottom), 17 (top left), 17 (top right), 17 (bottom left), 17 (bottom right), 18-19 (foreground), 18-19 (background), 24 (top left), 24 (bottom left); Dirk Ercken/Shutterstock Images, cover (bottom right), 20 (top right), 20 (bottom left), 20 (bottom right), 21 (top left), 21 (top right), 21 (middle left), 21 (bottom right); iStock/Thinkstock, 1; Natali Glado/Shutterstock Images, 3; Matt Gibson/Shutterstock Images, 5; Tracy Starr/Shutterstock Images, 6; Hugh Lansdown/Shutterstock Images, 9; Philip Yb/Shutterstock Images, 10 (right), 10 (middle); Paul J. Martin/Shutterstock Images, 17 (middle); Sascha Burkard/Shutterstock Images, 20 (top left), 21 (bottom left); Maks Narodenko/Shutterstock Images, 22-23; Parmoht Hongtong/Shutterstock Images, 24 (bottom right)

Produced for Amicus by The Peterson Publishing Company and Red Line Editorial.

Editor Jenna Gleisner
Designer Craig Hinton

Printed in Malaysia
HC 10 9 8 7 6 5 4 3 2 1
PB 10 9 8 7 6 5 4 3 2 1

The jungle is full of plants and animals. Let's see how many we can count!

1

One jaguar hunts. Jaguars hunt and live alone.

2

Two parrots eat nuts.
They crack them open
with their beaks.

3

Three sloths hang from trees. They spend most of their lives in trees.

4

Four green snakes
coil around trees. They
hold on with their tails.

5

Five marmosets sit on a log. They are the smallest monkeys in the world.

6

Six morpho butterflies fly by. They are one of the biggest kinds of butterfly.

7

Seven orchid plants grow.
They grow in every color
but black.

8

Eight large bats fly by. They are called flying foxes. They are the largest bats in the world.

9

Nine red-eyed tree frogs watch. Their red eyes scare larger animals away.

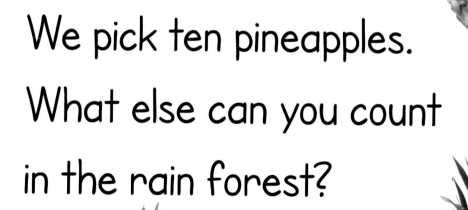

10

We pick ten pineapples.
What else can you count
in the rain forest?

Count Again

Count the number of objects in each box.